Beautiful

Chaos

Briipoetry©

TABLE OF CONTENT

For those who called themselves my "fans"
To those who believed in me,
inspired & motivated me to push forward & never
give up.
Thank you to those who caused me pain because
Without you this dramatism wouldn't exist.

[Elizabeth Gilbert]
"Ruin is a gift; ruin is the road to transformation"____
-Eat, Pray, Love

My life since I was a little girl has always been in ruins. It is only now that I have learned that with all the pain and the chaos we face in our lives, we can only grow from it. We have to see this ruin as a gift, as something that is helping to make us wiser and giving us the strength to face the truth in life. Ruin is the road to transforming our mind, body and soul. Without it we will be stuck in one spot, in one place with the same thoughts and the same outcomes. I have taken my pain and experiences and transformed them into words, into the only kind of poetry I can express for the world to understand. The only way I know how to communicate because verbal explanations were never my strong suit.
Here are the stages of my life…

<u>WHO I AM</u>

I am unique
I have an extraordinary physique
My darkness has reached its peak
and now I shine from beneath
Glory isn't always at the highest mountain
You can find it at the bottom of your feet
My pride tends to wallow to the floor but never breaks
Only rises from my fall
I am defined
My attitude catches crowds and fine comments always
intrigue my style
I am
Strong
Independent
I am known
Expand your atmosphere and enjoy my world
For I am not bleak
now let me introduce you to me

<u>INTRODUCING ME</u>

My breast may sag when not up right
My booty may jiggle if I don't do squats at night.
My hair's all messy if I don't tousle it fine
My makeup will smear if I don't straighten my line.
I have my flaws, but I clean up nice
just don't confuse my innocent look because I sure do
bite.
My thighs have dimples, I'm white all around
except for my nipples, they are wonderfully brown.
I have chubby toes and my lips are not plump but
you'll learn to love me in my entire funk.
I have scars for stories and tears to dry
But you'll never see me at my weakest bowing down
my pride.
My heart is full, my smile is kind
Why don't you try reading my book I'm sure you'll be
mystified.
I have curves for days my legs aren't long
once you get to know me my looks won't matter for
your throne.
I'm hot and I'm cold and that's just me
in finding perfection you might as well sleep.
Goodnight is a blessing and morning is a gift
stick with me and losing would only be a myth

<u>**WORDS**</u>

I write with every beat of passion
no hesitation on my actions
I flow through every letter with an easy pace
can't remember once I'm done
all these words spilled out for fun would soon erase
no need to fix the red line of these feelings
stories stay locked up in a cage trying to get away
chasing reality
time over mind slips away from my sanity
my seed plants the platform of homebody
my poetry has no mommy to nourish a dream to
spread
and I fall in defeat
but I feel the inspiration in my chest and my hand
refuses to rest
I continue to create my world
of black and blue

SEBASTYAN

Tickle, I tickle your little pudgy tummy
Giggle, you giggle your wide toothless mouth
the smell of your toes
how funky are those
but I am your mommy so ill swallow them whole
my heart beats with yours every breath you take
mommy and daddy are yours to deflate
my baby you are growing faster than the days
I'll cherish every moment, even in your rebellious
ways
I'll wipe up your tears and hold you close
why would I leave your side when you need me the
most
You're my rib, my heart and though you don't know
that
as many times as you drive me crazy
you're the reason for this joyous glow

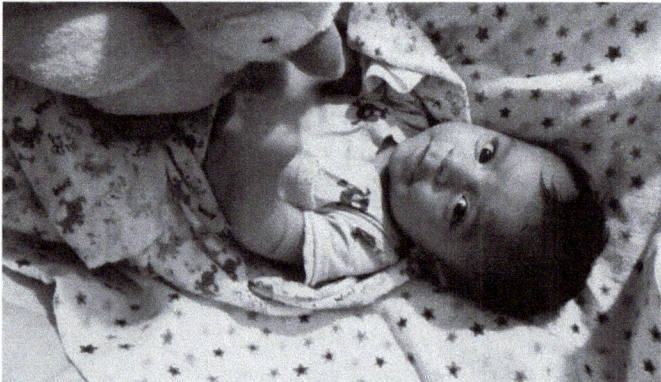

<u>MOTHER</u>

You hide behind words and smiles
You wouldn't look back
just kept running for miles
Portrayed your story of damsel in distress,
But when I climbed up to save you
I got pushed down,
No progress,
This two-faced action of immaturity has raised my
pride
You gave me motivation
you've boosted my drive
Now stay stuck in shrugs
face your foes,
life doesn't want a mother full of holes.

MOTHER OF LIES

You put me in a hole and kept me there to die
No care in the world if I wanted to survive
You gave me smiles and showed me glory
I never realized you were hiding the true story
You let me breath for moments at a time
When I wanted to linger you simply pushed me to the
side
Once I escaped and saw the inner demons
You kept denying the truth
you gave me cold hearted reasons
How dare you blame everything on me and never face
your foes
I never threw in your face you simply act like a hoe
You conjure up spells to keep your lovers around
Walk on the stone ground with your head held high
But I know your truth,
From your heart dying inside.

ATTACK

Bang!
Thud!
she ran in fear
Across the room he kept drawing near
They stopped and argued full of anger and hate
She hoped this would stop
before it was too late
The pain and sorrow have bled from her eyes
Showed all the love and romance that was between
them had died
Cuts and bruises seemed to travel above her veins,
The distance of love only emptied the drain.
Through all the suffer, and going insane
they finally saw an end
An ending with change…

<u>REMEMBER</u>

I can't remember my childhood but I remember the
pain
the stain left behind from a shard
running across my veins
hiding the split from my skin and bones
I remember the days that use to consume me whole
the darkened circles that covered my eyes
represented tears that could not hide
how dry my emotions to my fellow peers and yet deep
down inside
I was trying to scratch away all my fears
by and by years have come to pass,
more and more the dreading was seeming to last
I remember this light that held me tight and told me to
never fall apart
so I stood my ground fighting my battles of what
seemed to be endless loss
my scars healed up and now I am ready to cross
over to the clouds where I laid my heals,
This dramatic perfectionista has finally won her
ordeal.

BALANCE OF LOVE

Love isn't tender and kind,
it's not only swollen,
it's blind.
Love brings out many splendored things
but even so the consequences will always sting.
Pain and love are the strength and light to your soul,
It's the only way to keep you mentally and
emotionally whole.
Your blood needs to flow,
If there's no chaos,
then your heart will not grow.

<u>SEEKING</u>

I seek for imperfection
A dream of my reflection
I'm bounded in chains
by your love so true
I'm bounded in blame
from a heart confused
I seek for acceptance
life with no rejection
A time and place where I'm not thrown away from
you
Come hold me
your arms wide open
Come show me
dreams that are unbroken
Carry me into unspoken fields of wonderland
Make it real and hold my hand
I seek for redemption
a key for my infected heart
I seek for inception
stages of you and me never drifting apart.

<u>IN LOVE</u>

You're the reason my heart beats
whether fast or slow
My love for you has grown, you just don't know
I love you for all your flaws and fears; I'll make sure
never again will you shed
a single tear,
My morning my night every day of the week,
you're beautiful to me, even when you sleep
Your smile, your frown, your scent of all kinds
make me weak at the knees; please forever be mines.
Who can love you more than me?
I'll go beyond and back for you,
You never did believe me but I swear it's true.
I'll keep your face hurting from smiling so much and
make sure you shiver
from every inch of my touch.
I love you there's no question in that
let me show you forever just sit back and relax.
Raindrops fall one drop at a time,
lonely and fearless they let our sun shine
Flowers bloom yet fade the same; I swear I finished all
those foolish games
All memories that glowed they twinkle in your eyes,
dark shadows no longer cover our midnight sky
My darling, my dear how I love you so much,
don't want to lose your presence
want to lose your touch.

<u>FIRST LOVE</u>

These wounds, these scars
Still linger in my heart
Sore and swollen, pieces tend to fall apart
The beginning, in love is where it all starts
Crazy romance came at us like darts
Emotions were clear you took me by my pride
In the middle we fell, you believed I lied
Pushed me around, started to treat me like a side
Shoved me, closed me, filled me with lies
The fairy tale we lived in soon began to die
My world was turned upside down with your passion and
lust
My innocence, my life, all turned into dust
Love filled my body but began to blow me away
My head began to burst with your seductive ways
I poured out my eyes then they faded away
Even when I held you close, you still seemed like an
empty ghost
My heart tried to attacked your soul, bring you back
whole,
but you consumed me with a kiss,
then betrayed me with your sinful goals
This was an unfortunate miss,
I honestly thought this was final bliss
Now it is over and done
My first love was an experience I might never recover
from.

ABUSIVE LOVE GAME

Thrashed and abused
I slept my lonely nights away
You got cold and bitter day by day.
Missing your company
presence of divine beauty
I crawled back into the dark world
thinking I can become brand new.
With your verbal abuse of passion
I tried to transform my mind and soul
Into a better view for you
to see me reborn and whole.
Blood, sweat and tears
I drew for you
Life was endless
and without you my hopes were meaningless.
Screams for your love,
yet no heart came through
and the little love you gave me seemed to spill into blue.
Sadness, rage and greed was only in your eyes,
So you flung me around like a toy because of my lies.
No longer will I walk around with my head sunk down in shame
All because of an abusive love game.
Now you left me for good,
a single petal alone
My reddish glow is fading;
my sweet scent is no longer home.
The sun use to shine so bright helping my strength to grow,
And now only storms blow away my faith to show.
Clouds fluffier than my pillow,
I sleep under my weeping willow
And the ecstasy of excitement has gone
leaving me with only me.

~14~

CASE OF THE ABUSED HEART

You made me believe I was this devil spawn loser
when in reality you were the brother of his chooser.
Mind games had me in a daze
losing sight of my innocence I tried to remake.
My childhood was plentiful,
horrors and fears
when you came along
I thought I found the one to shake away all my
scarring years.
I felt as though you ripped out my heart and ate it with
your jaws
You'd laugh and smile and say "don't worry I love all
your flaws."
Foolish of me to believe you
all you did was run around and lie
while I sat in your dungeon and cried.
Blamed me for your insecurities
so you slept with others
denied me and replaced with your mistresses
left me with cruelty
this contagion in my heart.

DESPERATION

Stood those lonely nights lying in my bed
Just to hear your voice and rub your head
Cuddled your pillows and sheets
just to wrap your scent around my cheeks
I deal with your anger so biter and cold
Sincerity is all I have now, a changed heart from the past
All I beg for is another chance at your heart
a great love we once had
Now you push me away with all your doubts and fears
I pull you into my arms, my eyes soaked in tears
My head held low I sulk in my mistakes
you yell "FOREVER WILL NEVER BE US!", and I
continue to shake
I tell you "I'LL FIGHT FOR YOUR LOVE NO MATTER
WHAT IT TAKES"
you laugh and reply "YOUR NOTHING BUT A FAKE!"
I swing back and forth on a vine so thin
hoping it won't break and I'll finally win.
Your love and heart is all I'm asking but you won't stop
and listen, you're already packing.
I'm so sorry for being lost and confused
I never meant for our love song to turn into blues
I promise I changed; I'm yours till the end
but you're promising me never, Never ever again.

<u>FORGIVENESS?</u>

The scratches and scars upon your face
Never wanted to hurt you
just wanted your embrace
Begged and pleaded for you to stay
you did not want to listen, you stood far away.
I loved you and wanted you, never leave my side
Yet every time you came to me, I wanted to hide.
Wanted you to be my lover till death do us part
But we needed a beginning,
we needed a fresh start.
Cat and mouse, we played the game
As years passed by it never felt the same.
I'm sorry for everything I wish we could start over
You were my good luck charm
my four-leaf clover.
It killed me every day how sorry I was
Wish you could forgive me,
try and give a fuck.
I swear I'll keep you happy each day at a time
Just as long as I know I can call you mine.
I made the biggest mistake and I just want to take it back
The way I been wasn't a purpose act.
What hurts the most is that I lost my partner in crime
Figured I'll let you breathe,
give us some personal time.
I need a way to relax
I need to blow off some steam
Cried too many tears
yet they meant nothing to you
Just want us to laugh and play just like we use to.

THE LONELY SINNER

Tragedy hit the lonely sinner
Smiles fade away,
they no longer shimmer
Closer and closer the lights get dimmer
Shadows all around me,
my heart beats thicker
Pouring from my chest my heart forms a river
Slowly they peel away
casting bolts to my shiver
Knelt down I pray
for these trembles to go away
Prayer's twirling around my head
laughing as they linger
Cloud 9 hit my head;
tossed me back down for being a lonely sinner

PIT OF DESPAIR

Fell backwards into a pit
thought to pull myself but I laid there in my ditch
Rolled around in the mud I thought would clean my
slate
Only realizing after that so many falls was my fate
Head up to the sky I'm soaring mighty high traveling
past my mind, confused
with the reality I called mine
My own breaking future I sought out the truth;
nirvana
but only pain was my fountain of youth.

<u>BURIED</u>

In denial of one's true self,
lonely thoughts of painful submission
Circular motions got me dizzy and dry,
cold tears only drill me to stay alive
I've left my stories to bury in the sand
but still, I walk on these hidden strands
How tight my chest when I let loose in the wild,
I suffocate even more because I tied my pride to the
ground
how shameless it is to scream **FUCK THE WORLD**!
But who do you know that will literally change the
world?
in the depths of passion, I cradle the pain away,
I let my longing linger even when the sun strays away.

FED UP

I'm over the abuse,
Pettiness of others,
I'm tired of being blamed for something for someone else's shit,
I'm tired of being hushed and having to close my mouth.
I'm just tired of my negative life.
So, fuck it all it's time for change.
Now I get rid of negativity and surround myself with positivity
and it may take a while but that's ok because only from the bottom is where
you will rise to the top. ----
So sick of excuses the bullshit and lies.
Tired of "I can't" or "I'm going to try".
I need,
I will
and I'm doing it now.
I need love unconditional,
have it spewing from your lips caressing my mind and tormenting my hips.
I can't afford no more "ok's" and I "Know's",
I need more of "I got you no problem" and then that's the ends of the show.
Fuck the drama and the mountains we climb,
because at the end of it all it is the triumph of victory we will find.

I need more than "I'm trying my best", because I'm
over the
disappointments
I crave the passion from within with no fear to put it
in motion.
The devotion from your touch and the fire from your
stare is what I need to
keep my lungs filled with air.
Damn do I need penetration, not only sexually but in
the heart, from there
That's where the family grows, we keep it tight and
we won't ever fall
apart.
I'm just a woman in need, someone who's been
rejected from a seed and
now that I'm wiser all I want is what belongs to me.

<u>I YELLED</u>

I yelled
Silence fell over the town
they're kryptonite
despite the torment that came over you
I yelled
but liberty bell was of no use.
Government shot me down miles off the road
Told the public and I stumbled
On my own,
all alone.
Symbols around my head
I cradled in my bed,
letting propaganda destroy your minds
I yelled
Silence fell
And yet no words subsided my hell.

OPEN YOUR EYES

Open your eyes see what's inside,
these hidden words that beautify.
Don't you see what lies beneath
isn't exactly what we call reality?
This mystical road is only fairytale,
our lullaby to get us by
Open your eyes to what flies past the stars
that twinkle above your head and puts you to bed,
that hypnotize your eyes and dream what is to be
dead.
They give you this imaginary wonder of fun and
games
when truly it is you that gets lost in your brain
Open your eyes to these subliminal lies
only to take over your life and treat you like a slave
without you realizing you need to be saved.

THE WORLD IS A MESS

The world is a mess
the future seems so stressed
a mind full of chaos
people counting their checks
Trying to survive in this life by drinking or cyphe
blinded by the man, confusing the lost with symbolic
bands
we're confused by the beats skipping along in the
streets
holding on to your pride driven mad by the money
tide
How long can we go closing our eyes while hell
unfolds?
We should rise and unite chasing the stars as we ride
the fright
paint a picture so brand new
share those eyes with someone true
build mountains out of air
Undivided and unfair
the world is distressed
We need guidance, we are blessed
love each other and renew all the lives you bumped
into
Inside humans are all the same
created equal with no shame
just because we quarantined the things unknown

in the end we are all creators to the spread of
corruption worldwide
The demons we share instill this fear we all bare
power that's gained drains the goodness once held
high in the game

CONTROL

I need a way to release my mind
Control this time
I fear I have no way of letting go
With the beats drumming closer
I look over my shoulder
And I see that the shadows keep creeping near
Try to defeat the order
Run from this bulldozer
And open my eyes to reality
I need to slow down these emotions
Concrete these commotions
Of the mind control that will bring us all to fear

JUST THOUGHTS

I hold back tears
Just to try and defeat my longing fears.
My anxiety likes to tickle my nerves,
just makes me want to fall down and curl up into a
ball.
Stressed about what?
Life?
Just life
What more can I ask for?
so, all I do is cyphe.
Still damaged by old flings
now this new one keeps bringing old demons in.
I hold myself back from upcoming dreams,
Knowing my potential but reality hits me
shows me these unfortunate things,
My heads lost
my hearts tossed,
Just broken into pieces
walking without a straight destination to grow.

CYPHE

Cyphe my life in the air I breathe
Do you see the pain, the ultimate stain?
Blow it away to the sky and unwind
let the damages pass by and clear the tides.
Tilt my head back and close my eyes
blunt in hand now I'm really alive.
Fuck those tears I'll keep them choked in my throat
high in my mind I watch all my emotions float.
Time just stopped a minute or two
now I dominate my world
a vision brand new.

THE RESURRECTION

You laugh and giggle with your crooked smile
I love the way you tease me with your wacky style
U lifted me off my feet
only to fly with me to the clouds
Where a whole new world was brought to me
and structured my miles
I thought it was over,
this ride called humiliating life
just dropped out and blew down my cyphe
you came along grabbed me by the hand
said to me "don't worry baby, let me put u to a stand"
cradled my fears and recovered the broken seams
now we begin the life of resurrecting my dreams

<u>I OPENED</u>

I walked the glazing path
Only smiles took a hold of my face
Inside I grew strong
Full of grace
I made my way in with one easy pace
Behold it's nearby,
the future entwined,
from my shadow to the light
It was no longer suicide

<u>SECOND LOVE</u>

You've shown me light when the clouds caved in,
I love the rain but you brought me in
Snuggled me close
your heat tickled my nose
You assured me peace from those lying foes
The goof has won; a big heart fills your soul,
I can't believe happiness was built on this love so
slowly.

MY LITTLE BUMBLE BEE

My flower my nectar
so juicy to the lips,
I'll suck up your vector and blow you a kiss
Sting life with a gift
so romantic and clean,
I'm your yellow sunshine and I can barely be seen.
You'll grow full of lilies,
roses and buds
My flower my nectar
I'll provide your field with love.

<u>LOVE BUG</u>

I stopped and stared
Who is this man?
His gaze like a flame,
those words knowing how to tame
A woman like me Seeks for desire and passion
This man that approaches shows me fire and satisfaction
The tattoos up and down his arms got me working up an
appetite
His fingers when they touch me,
Gets me all bothered and hot
when he kisses me, it really hits the spot
He has those lips like gummy bears
Keep on teasing me with that seductive stare
Am I worthy for your love?
I've been rejected so many times, I can't remember that
bug
I stopped and sighed
Finally, a man who won't leave my side
Blessing me and increasing my pride
I will no longer hide
You've helped me to defeat the destruction inside
No longer the cries, you are my drive
And now I'll rise
with the deliverance of this love bug that invaded my
heart,
Was once suicide.

NATURE'S BEATS

Those cotton candy skies in my eyes
Make me smile brighter than the sun
It's the breeze hitting the trees that release the steam
Surrounding my dreams
I wish I was a bee sucking life's sweet nectar
Flying high and free away from the traffic below
I'll jump on every flower drinking the juices of pure
love
Feeling light from a petal
I'm reborn, brand new
Every whistle of my kiss would echo and send chills
to the moon
How tranquil the waves that massage my feet
All over these wavelengths send rhythms to the
creatures beneath
Tickling my toes, the fish swim with glee
Hypnotizing my mind wishing I could escape under
the sea
When the sun sets and night time approaches
I sigh from all that twinkles in such a graceful motion
How elegant you dance across the midnight sky
My eyes always get heavy from your whisper
lullabies
I travel through time with every shooting star I see
I shudder with goose bumps, as the wind invades the
peace in me

The crickets around chime passed my ears
Soft melodies linger calming all my fears
I beg God for this feeling to forever last
I dare not face my mourning past
Until I awake to deal with the crowded streets,
Let me linger a while and marinate with nature's
simple beats.

ICE CREAM

You're bad for me
Got my senses fleeing from me
These cavities
Show no mercy to my greed
My brain freezing
Makes my heart beat fast and slow
Confusing me
From these feelings forming below
Only to catch my breath, hold me tight and never let
go
Show me what's been missing and make my spirits
glow
Come tell me time and time again how much you love
me so
You're just like ice cream
Slowly moving down my throat
Chilling all of my intestines inside
You're just like ice cream
Hugging the taste buds on my tongue
Electrifying my crime
I simply can't understand this, how can something so
messy feel so right
I'm not sure of what to feel
Your crazy flavors seem unreal
Got me freezing to my heel
You're just like ice cream
I'm infected

Got me restless
I can't lie
Baby kiss me one more time before I cry
Got me hot
Got me cold
Got these flavors blasting melodies, tingling my nose
Got me hip
Chocolate chip
Swirls of pinks and reds cover my face
Only now I'm turning blue
So flavalicious falls on you
Berry me something brand new
You're just like ice cream
I'm infected
Got me breathless
I won't lie
Let me kiss you one more time before I die

THE GOOD & THE BAD

Seduction
Manipulation
2 things both good and bad
yet I desire them both
The balance of life only intoxicates me and draws me
closer to the mysteries
of both heaven and hell
Good vs. Evil
What desires lie within
when my reality is so misunderstood
I have several confusions scratching at my throat
clawing its way out of my skin.
What to do
how to control the madness of my truth
while I suffer my daily life
of lies and pain.

<u>SEX</u>

Shortness of breath and chest so tight
How could we ease our breathing with this love
making fight?
You pulled me down your rabbit hole of fun
But even as I cried out
tightness filled my lungs
Oh, how my body shivers with satisfaction,
every stroke made my skin melt beneath your touch
Our only reality was our cruel world of lust
and the deeper you got in me the closer I wanted to
bust
Now with our marks of love seeming so complex,
let's go again
another round of endless unwanted sex.

<u>BLOW</u>

Come blow my mind
One lick at a time
Come blow these trees
Beneath my knees
I feel the shutter
From every drop
How white the stain
Just eased my pain
Come blow a kiss
With ultimate bliss
Now feel the fall
Underneath these draws

<u>ALL NIGHT</u>

I stay up thinking
Boy you been teasing me for way too long
I been hoping, while I'm smoking
You'd drop to your knees invade me please
You got me broken, you burst me open
Baby don't fight this feeling
I want you right now
You know you want this
Show me what you got
You be hittin that spot
all night
You woke up with my berry all in your mouth
Juicy and tight
Feeling nice from all this cyphe
Can't keep me eyes off ya papi
Do me right,
drop that pipe
You got me hypnotized with every bite
Love me all night
Last thing I remembered is our wet silky bodies
slipping and sliding in the tub
Let's reach our climax
While rolling all over these sheets
Got me tongue tied within our beats
Your sweat dripping all over me
Rubbing on me, rubbing on my booty

Got my heart pumping
Now ride me slow down to the floor
Got me at my peak I'm feeling weak
I'm melting on you
all night

UNEXPECTED

It blew my mind how we got lost in time,
But it never occurred to me
how you were always mine.
We flew the world and watched it all pass us by,
We only stopped to sit back
and sigh.
Our moments filled the air
while love was just sinking in
and I couldn't catch a beat with my heart racing thin.
Our sins now rest to bed
while we hold each other tight
I smile upon my love
sleeping away the starry night.

<u>CAVED</u>

I caved in
dove in deep
I left the Sheppard my soul to keep
I'm backwards
I'm upside down
Confused about the motion
You've inflicted upon my crown
I shed hard
I bled fast
Only once could you control
The demons you've grasped

THE "WORD"

You use the word so much
in my chest the feeling lost its touch
How valuable each letter used to be
spreading it loosely across the sea
Now the lies suffocate the flow
and my heart falls apart for the time and energy spent
protecting the beauty
in a word...

~41~

STAND UP, BREAK FREE

I feel sorry for the days you left abused,
walking around head low blaming self-accused.
Misguided emotions flying back and forth from once
a muse
now left shattered and alone because of a short fuse.
Don't let them knock you till your pride is fucked up
and confused,
show your true self-worth
stand up and release your juice,
don't let anybody tell you your hearts an aching joke,
just saddle up and take a ride on your epic float.
Once, twice, three times they hit,
I would've swung right back with the words of my
biblical spit, only one man
has the right to judge me as a whole,
and can nobody sit here and try to diminish my soul,
I can love and live everywhere I go,
but don't mistake my kindness for weakness.
who thinks they're bigger than GOD himself?
needs to check in the mirror again stop denying your
true self.
Love yourself
and be happy in life,
conquer the world and defeat your greatest fight.

~42~
<u>NEW YEARS</u>

Happy new years from me to you
may all your wishes and blessings come true.
Smile at the people who made you laugh,
love those even more who have led you down the
wrong path.
For even if evil has met your eye,
May you be kinder and wise this new year to come
and hope we all just get together and have some fun.
Let's cry for the passing year
for the wrong we have done
and keep the fights behind us because now we have
won.
We can reminisce about the past and morn for those
who didn't last,
but now it's time to turn the page and celebrate our
New Year's birth to our up-and-coming age.
Happy new years to all with a great big kiss and hug,
How I hope this year will bring us nothing but joyful
love.

OLD FLAME

you defined your time with boldness and sass
once upon a time you were quiet and bash
our memories of love and lust now shadow present
thoughts
don't stir up old feelings for my fragile heart will
pounce fast
distance between us got me losing sleep
wondering what's cradling beneath the deep
I've inhaled the memory of your skin so sweet
the color of caramel melting from my lips to my feet
now you have my body on overheat
my pussycat purring
tingling all the nerves that seemed lost to me
my confusing stranger
you held my heart so close
Who are you now?
What do you desire the most?

<u>HOW DO YOU...</u>

How do you tame the waves from crashing against
your walls?
and even if it is unsteady, you're just waiting for the
fall.
How do you tame the wounds and not sink into the
deep....

CREATURES OF THE NIGHT

I feel the pain, but I won't complain,
Touching my body bounded by shackled chains
Don't release the peace
The chaos is so bittersweet
Let's not strengthen our defeat but marinate in the
beat of our broken feet
Collapse into each other as creatures of the night
Our climax so forbidden
Drowning out our fearful doubts
I've blind flooded my senses to enjoy what seems
unknown
But you've uncovered me
Deep throated all your passions filling every hole
Does it make sense?
Did I suck the juices from your brain?
Our mind fuck will put your love making to shame
As we indulge in the panic of lust
Biting into the rhythm of the music and what remains
is the stain of our names engraved in our hearts.

THE BITE

I bit into a moment so deep
my heart pounded so hard
it didn't miss a beat.
Infatuation so pure
My longing for lust traced your back as I clawed.
Passion burst bluntly from your core
You didn't care if your body was sore
just kept going for more
We let our juices trickle and pour to the floor
And as u held me tight, I inhaled this beauty,
for only tonight will I submit to your cockiness truly.
You growled at my seductive sight
Leaving drools at my feet
switching Dom overnight.

<u>VAMPIRE</u>

Catch me,
I'm gliding over your head
Passing gently
I let you ravish me till my body's dead
Trap me,
grab my wrists
Let the cold drip off the wall and trickle past my hips
Seduce my clothes with your earnest mouth
Lacing me with your growth,
I milky way down south
Please me
tease me
keep me in a daze
Your true blood instincts kept my heart pumping for
days
Sub me to the floor while you domed my every move
Screams and moans kept us dancing,
bodies grooving to the moon
Bite my lips for thy master
as he watched in delight
The end didn't seem near us,
this vampirism sight.

～48～
<u>HIGH</u>

She wanted the high of those frequencies blowing her
mind
She reached for the sky her clit so soft and powerful
she opened wide
He spread her lips and slid in penetrating her blind
What lust, was it love for her soul?
How much could she gain?
Build up from her toes they shivered in sweat from
this game
Sweet and sour to the core they exploded in names
Collapsed in the arms of a man that was bounded in
chains
Never hers to be freed
It was all just a play for the taste
That white sticky feeling which filled up her holes
was the paste
She searched for the high
Until one man could deliver her break
From the fire in her eyes that would lead to her fatal
fate.

<u>LOST PASSION</u>

Never said I wasn't true
I understand that I messed up but I feened for you
King and queen roles we played but now our fires
through
No more light to ignite these passions that burned past
the feud
How do we cope with mediocre hope to keep our
reign afoot?
Now we lay with such dismay
Fighting the tides that kill our heartfelt waves
I don't feel for you
Our wounds were stitched but now they are seeping
blue
So down and out from misguided mouths
Was this love even true?
How do we put together the bubble that popped
forever?
With this strain of revitalizing our pain of pleasure
I thought I knew ways to make a change to rearrange
the trials life has given to you
I don't feel for you
Love is blind and so is time
So, let's start anew.

~50~
I GOT YOU

When the sun is gone, I can hear you cry
But baby I'm not home to be by your side
I'll make my way to you
one stop maybe two
To keep you on your feet
I'll be your solace and peace
My love let's munch away
all these fears and pains
And I will cry with you
to show I love you too
It will be ok
Let's laugh the night away
Dry these tears on your face
come into my warm embrace
Ill chase the world to be with you
No amount of time will keep me from being with you
I'll ride the waves to make sure I see this through
These memories won't last long
So no shame
Don't blame yourself for the fuse
because release will only rejuvenate you.

<u>BACK AT IT</u>

I have good days I have bad days
Sometimes I'm all smiles and other days I just want to run for miles
On the outside I hide my marks of pain yet on the inside I'm so full of self-blame
My minds at a thousand and I can't breathe
Days I lay still hoping I'm still able to heal

<u>WAVES</u>

I remember the times we had are now slipping to the
shore
Watched the waves crashing against the rocks like we
were making love on the floor
All the distance we spent trying to silence the roars
And the war we've cast because we slipped from our
chores
All the smiles given completely covered hells doors
Now we sink to the bottom of that ocean floor

<u>TRUTHS</u>

Deceitful eyes hide behind a contagious smile
But you separated our souls by your continuous lies
You held me close with your stroking force
And hypnotized reality onto a lust filled course
Divided in terror
I tried to keep this ride lasting forever
But swollen in pain
I closed my eyes to the shame
Your seed penetrated another, manipulated by drugs
and a former lover
Now I shed my sorrows on the floor
With all these truths barging at my door
Anxiety weighing me down
But fuck if I walk around with a frown
If only pleases me to know that this karma feud will
take its toll
We all get screwed but we all blossom too
But I died in the arms of a man who confused my
truths

<u>DEPRESSION</u>

Depression keeps scratching at door
tickling my soul while it screams NO MORE!
Slowly and slowly my heart grows weary
my smile stays bright but my eyes seem dreary.
As they shine light brown bliss,
you'd never think to look at what stains these lips.
From kisses to sex, nothing seems to fill this void.
If only I can download an app to kill these monsters
on my android.
I'll eat and eat to kill this pain,
not realizing the pounds that I've purposely gained;
so with the weight I'll frown even more
inventing insecurity to close all my doors.
Bored out of my mind and growing insane,
I've only wanted love to diminish this pain.

THE END

She was afraid to let it show
All the feelings left unknown
To all your eyes
She was alive
Though she walks with these hidden lies
All alone beneath her skin
She was drowning from deep within
Yet all the yearning bleeding through
You never thought she needed you
Now she lies in a pool of blood
She couldn't help but release the love
And now she sleeps with grime's kiss
One note to explain the stain upon her wrists
Full force
One slit
Was all there was to quit
Into the light to defeat the night
While peace surrendered
To hold her tight
Goodnight.

‘*NO FILTER motions of a poet*’

Was origionally the title I wanted this book to be. I saw it as me being open & raw. Over the years I've learned that I am truly *Beautifully Chaotic* & well…arent we all? We live in a world of survivors, fighters & artists who express themselves in so many different ways. I express myself with Love, Lust & Poetry.

Throw me into the ocean
& let me breathe the salty air
the bubbles are my translation
for a different love affair.

FOR MORE CONTENT
[IG: BRIIPOETRY]
[SCAN ME]

@BRIIPOETRY

ISBN 979-82-18-42125-0

www.ingramcontent.com/pod-product-compliance
Lightning Source LLC
Chambersburg PA
CBHW070012100426
42741CB00012B/3213